Don't Order the Calamari

Poems by Rob Azevedo

Kung Fu Treachery Press
Rancho Cucamonga, CA

Copyright © Rob Azevedo, 2021
First Edition: 1 3 5 7 9 10 8 6 4 2
ISBN:978-1-952411-87-8
LCCN: 2021950623

Cover image: Brendan McCormick
Author photos: Michael A. Brooks,
All rights reserved. No part of this publication may be
reproduced or transmitted in any form or by any means,
electronic or mechanical, including photocopying,
recording or by info retrieval system, without prior
written permission from the author.

Acknowledgements:

The author would like to thank the editors at DumpFire Press and allpoetry.com where some of these poems have previously appeared (in one form or another).

Special thanks to Brendan McCormick, Michael A. Brooks and Kung Fu Treachery Press.

Table of Contents

Bowl of Destiny / 1

You Own Me / 2

Gagging on Cold Cuts / 3

Lay Heavy On My Skin / 5

He Rises Unfed / 6

Fogged Over / 7

It's Go Time! / 8

Motionless On The Side Of the Road / 9

Giddy Nymphs / 10

So Do We, Baby / 11

The Tumble / 13

Cutting Through The Current / 15

I Will Follow / 16

Fiends / 17

The Grain It Leaks / 19

Heaven's Sweet Delight / 20

I Fell For It / 21

Lift Your Brow / 23

Songs Of Regret / 25

Grazing Like A Sow / 27

Brotherhood Broken / 29

Shallow Grave Of Secrets / 30

Making My Way Towards Nowhere / 31

Loud and Wide / 32

Too Fast Too Soon Too Much / 33

Lather My Bones In Tar / 35

Don't Order The Calamari / 37

Words Just Can't / 380

Happy To Share / 40

Sprung From A Funk / 41

Hush and Wait / 42

Paunchy Pony Boy's (for Johnny) / 43

To Do With Kindness / 45

Pockets of Flesh / 46

Broken Shadows / 48

Wet My Gullet / 49

Hijacked at Night / 50

To Be Heard / 52

Yes, sir. / 53

Train Wreck / 55

Expectations / 56

Pig Skinner / 57

I Say So / 58

Back Of The Buggy / 60

The Beautiful Unknown / 62

Fraught With Treachery / 63

And Then We Tango / 64

Rolling Force Of Fungi / 65

From Bing to Pavarotti / 66

Burning Down The Tower / 67

Dedicated to the Gang at allpoetry.com

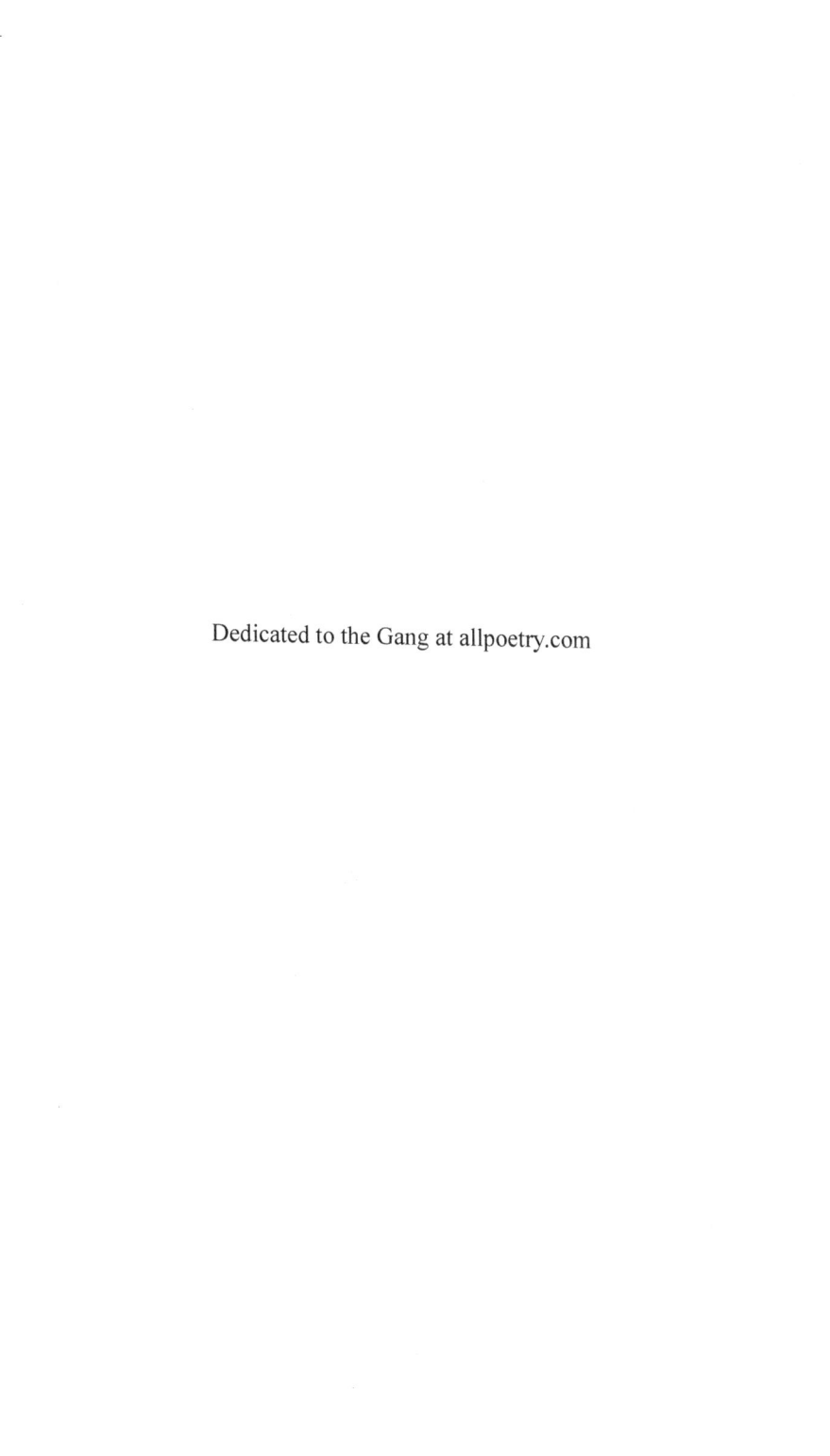

Searchin' high, searchin' low
Searchin' everywhere I know
Askin' the cops wherever I go
Have you seen dignity

-Bob Dylan

BOWL OF DESTINY

you stood silently
bent slightly toward
the burrowing glare of dusk,
aglow in an orange gaze,
your laced legged garments
greeted by a million sleeping stars
cascading in full whispers,
grinding songs of want
of friction
of deliverance
against the edge of darkness
whilst my innards burst
into flames
and my fingers twitch
and my teeth,
dry to a squeak,
convulse and churn beyond
the tongue,
now wagging like a mutt,
frothing almost
on bowls of loneliness,
seated at the thrown
of destiny.

YOU OWN ME

Aching to taste the heel of your foot,
your crumpled brow,
the lineage of your stamina,
I wrangle my might
and set forth
unrepentant, unmade, unwashed
and crowd my mind with
the blowing scent of
browning thighs
that shine and tumble
on slippery ground,
whipping down hard on my
electric loins,
our tongues tied like rat tails,
tangled and swollen,
deserted by starry skies,
digested by lust,
exposed with weakness,
as cloudy drops of sweat
meander down the nape
of your neck,
down the line of your spine,
into the stacked flesh
dimpled and screaming for touch.

You own me.

You know it.

And I am good with that.

GAGGING ON COLD CUTS

same routine, same thoughts
most circling around a woman
with wide hips
or a bent hose-covered knee
or the dizzying hint of an areola
brazenly displayed in the cold cut aisle.

these thoughts, this routine,
fully encrusted, each of them,
fanged in spots with silver tips,
spouting words forgotten
by Kings and Queens.

these barren crusted thoughts
arrive steady as the evening news,
ridden upon the backs of
frauds and finks,
as the long-eared beaters
cough and gag on the night
from the street outside my window.

these thoughts,
these thoughts,
these thoughts,
always circling the drain,
spiraling down in a cascade
of deliberate brutishness,
vain with gummed up wisdom,

constricted by need,
consumed with lust,
as these thoughts shop for eggs and bread
peering unseen into the blouses
of firm breasted strangers
standing over bargain meats,
measuring their might
against my own.

LAY HEAVY ON MY SKIN

A crushing glance
glowing beyond recognition
lays heavy on my skin
as piles of bent twisted rays
spring fast across
my hung dried neck
weathered pockets of gloom
abandoned by dabs of light
languishing on riverbeds
on mountainsides
on matted sands flooded with pennies
and rings of constellations
pairing peacefully
on the crystal shores
sliding sideways against
my hangdog grin.

HE RISES UNFED

your veiny eyes said it all
worn out orbs of misgivings
slender in their appeal
guarded under lock and key
yet televised on the big screen
the nomadic waif
curled into himself
long after dawn with only winks of light
flattened against each angled breath
the man barks at the Gods
his innards scrambled with bacon grease
bloody eyed and brooding
lips peeled clean of meat
he lunges into himself
into the ghosts
long past graceful
and rises unfed
to meet the day.

That is, if I was staring.

FOGGED OVER

The glint in my eye fogs over
as the meat of my hands
begin to rumble.

The rustling started in my chest, that
rambling, hollow, slow rolling emotion
that stinks of disease, trucked its way into
my elbows and neck, which has tightened
as each minute of the show clicks by.

Ruined by the human condition,
exhausted with lust, these trumpets
spit blood at the hungry crowd,
baiting the savages to widen
their tongues.

For blood, for revenge, for sport.
The rich, the brooding, the warped
scramble like hounds to cry into
the eyes of each victim, scorched
and torn with cruel intention.

The taste of dead fish captures
my senses, that ruinous aftertaste
melds its way into my candor, lacing
the hours in knotted anxiousness.

It's all too much -- the betrayal,
the contempt, the flaming minds
that swell with indifference.

IT'S GO TIME!

two sticks of dynomite
to ram up this greasy beasts nostrils.

a hefty double-barrel flare gun
pointed at his 90-inch monster neck.

a bow knife to slice into his fiery innards
walled thicker than the Prudential Center.

two bear traps to suck and snap
his pillar ankles as I chock him
with barbed wire.

a massive net to swallow his claws and fanged teeth
so I can break them off -- one by one --
and ram them into his yellow eyeballs.

a wailing tongue to burn his black ears
and melt a fist-full of wax soon fed into
his deep wallowing wounds.

and steel fists to beat the drum of his hammer chest
as I knee his grotesquely triumphant testicles to dust.

for dessert, I slice off his bodacious nipples
and fry them to perfection
in a stolen skillet.

Salt and butter not included.

MOTIONLESS ON THE SIDE OF THE ROAD

what began as a high jinks adventure
veered off into chaos,
a blackened state of affairs
where the wild winds of Wichita
conquered the swelling night
and lay trembling wires of mischief
upon our leather skirts,
now crusted over
with quivering tears
falling flat upon baited cheeks
as the blackened night
dominated our dispositions
an incomprehensible longing for home
stood motionless on the roadside
as we thumbed our way through the
invisible haze of hopelessness
and shuffled lost on sickly knees
our feet heavy as timber,
our eyes hooked with fear
we traveled on the winds
cursed with swollen swagger,
as we ached for the smell
of our Father's faces.

GIDDY NYMPHS

Dagger-faced dilatants with a penchant
for perversion rattle his screen door
and trample his roses, sending his cats
scurrying under empty bottles of wine,
spilling over ashtrays filled with limp smokes.

The writer hides under the bed, steaming
from every pore, last nights load a blackened
shadow wading in forgetfulness.

The underdog rubs at his bloated acid gut
and fingers his thinning hairline
with magic yellow wands
as the giddy nymphs line his walkway
with spiral notebooks
filled with gibberish, aching to taste
Hanks bulbous nose and lay waste
to his working days,
now drowned out in adulation.

A poet's greatest enemy.

SO DO WE, BABY

better days ahead, she says,
as the lying gimp fades into
another dying smoke
bending across her fingers.

you played me, you fink, I said,
with your dented smile and
weather torn cleavage.

you're weak, she reminded me,
a whiny sod with holes in your face.

you slag, I told her, you rotten,
strung out, puss infested user.
i told you you were filthy.

how dare you!
you, you...you celebrated phony.
so content to pass your perversions off as art.

how dare me! i loathe your
battered face and foggy breath.
death to your loins!

the waiter comes over.

care for another drink, folks?

yes, good sir.
make my woman's a double.
she deserves the best of everything.

thanks, baby. need another smoke?

nah, babe.
this one still has some life in it.

so do we, baby.

so do we.

THE TUMBLE

Humility is about
acceptance
not just of oneself
but for all people.

A trait worth celebrating
where each rock rolls
unwittingly askew,
some through ditches
and cracks filled
with mud,
while others saunter
downward,
fingering daisies
and soft beds of snow
and into the crystal face
of a sandy riverbed,
yet the tumble
is mimicked since
the dawn of time,
where some are flat,
some have curves,
some are just there
to spiral towards fate,
marble smooth.

we all stop
we all roll
we chip in spots
and no one shines
the same hue,
but it's the trip
through the roots
and vines,
through the puddles
and scabbed trees
that gives us reason enough
to celebrate.

CUTTING THROUGH THE CURRENT

These moments
when alone
covered in hot flesh
delirious with desire
owning my lust
that burns deep in
crystalized holy spots,
my mind swims
with wanton hands
fingering the edges
of my heat,
as I dive
headlong into
a trance
and tease
and cover
and reach
for your
salty taste
only to find you
miles away
cutting through
the sharp currents
with some other
lover.

I WILL FOLLOW

Still,
I would wrap my thoughts
around your pipeline dreams
and meld into your sonatas.
Regardless of our bloodlines
I would bend at every curve
to straighten your broken thoughts.
I would call on your day of birth
and shower you with plenty
because your smile balloons my spirts.
I would cry into your chest
when my core begins to melt
as the air gives way to dust.
And always, I would languish
in your minutia and follow you
through every fantasy.
Still
and always
and beyond
I will follow you all.

Because
That's what we do.

FIENDS

these rank bastards
keep feeding off
my deliberations,
angling for my spine,
for my spirit,
for my freedom
and notebooks
as I launch hell-bent
through the poisoned
brambles,
cutting past the swine
and the forgotten,
past the weird
and wasted,
each sucking on tabs
of mescaline,
drunk on rot gut,
drunk on lies,
sick with denial,
these crucified souls
nailed
to the amendments in which
they ridicule.
Bastards!
All of them!
loveless sods
bred by motherless
grunts,

these dying dreamers
screwing my knees into
Iris' "Wasteland of the Free"
as I roar half-mad
through the mountainside
cranked up on madness
as the Stones
as Jefferson Airplane
as Steppenwolf
rip my ears from
my skull
and remind me
that only the strong
make it out alive.
Fiends!
Each of you!
I'll shit down your throat
on your deathbed
as I read Hemingway
and smoke an antler pipe
and lap at a dead bottle of rye
until the sun breaks
until the music ends
until the swine die
on splintered crosses.

THE GRAIN IT LEAKS

the grain it leaks
all at once,
'tween these midnight
winks
and cross town
love affairs,
this coat of desperation
that widens and cools
as bits of hollow wit
bend with grains of grit
lapping at the seeds of
our confusion,
now rank with delusion,
begging for seclusion,
their mind boarded
from inclusion,
with hot loins that gather dust
amongst the traders
and the finks,
the liars and their winks,
each bludgeoned with waste
with lust not trust
and skin
rough as stone.

HEAVEN'S SWEET DELIGHT

Glom onto my waist
my wrists
my teeth
and drag me to
your lighthouse of love
where the winds cross wide
against molten skies
and shimmers against
the blinding waste
bubbling
at my feet --
long, viscous pools
of a sinister past,
strangling the roots of posies
and the weeds
and the licking flames
of my bitter plight
to prosper as a cheat,
as a heathen,
as a sinner,
as my eyes of dung
blink with sin
and reach sullenly
for the honey sweet taste
of heavens
earned delights.

I FELL FOR IT

Others have tempted me
with horizons, that grizzled land
of loyalty,
hand-picked with stony contradictions.

And I fell for it.

Others have swam with me
in pools of glass
and called it crystal,
then tied my ankles with jawbones
and watched me sink.

And I fell for it.

Others have promised me towers of love,
long gaping passages of passion
and patience,
then beckoned me to the gallows
to suffer in advance.

And I fell for it.

Others have tempted me with flesh,
that slow roasted heat bomb of
toxicity,
then introduced themselves as Judas
reincarnated.

And I fell for it.

Then there was you,
sitting in plain sight,
a butterfly ensconced in tribal
delirium, touching down
with ink-stained wings
to promise me nothing
but companionship --
Not loyalty
Not passion
Not promises.

Just friendship.

So, I fell for it.

LIFT YOUR BROW

lift your brow
up out of the gutter
and sniff the mornings
bitter wine.

roll your tongue
against the breeze
then slide headlong
into a new beginning.

bathe in the marrow
of the noonday sun
before you slice
at the stalks
that shade you.

then feast on dusk's
burning embers
and feed the night
with rivers of gold
that cling to shores
that hold you.

Free Me
this bag of stones
these humbled sacks
drink from the vines
that feed me

this stony place
in which i walk
covered in brine and
river thorns
reach for my face
too seize me

this body encased
in metal stains
sharp to the touch
with rusted proof
of a life betrayed me

this weeping face
dried in exile
dazing at the ruins
while counting stars
that abandoned me

the shiny spots
that break at the tip
and beckon me
to the gallows
to free me

SONGS OF REGRET

I have a friend
he writes songs
good ones too
drinking
trucker tunes
and he cheats
on his woman
and now he's
full of regrets
and nostalgia
and he thinks
as he festers
in his humility
if he writes
more songs
and plays the
hobo
and drives by
his lady's house
she might come out
and beg him
for another song
but she never does
so now he sings
lost love songs
to himself.

And no matter
how sorrowful
the words are
how bleak his days are
she ain't coming back.

They rarely ever do.

GRAZING LIKE A SOW

As a sow might,
my goal is to graze,
to graze about on
spoons full
with tobacco spit
laced with fish oil
as the wisps
of my thinning hair
dangle in the thickets,
nesting in the deep cut
willows where supple
mouths meet my gaze
over soggy flames
possessed with
contentment and reason,
as a mob of doers
gather in the square,
surrounding me with
turmoil, crawling up
my spine,
bending thorns into
my willingness to revel
in the mixed delight
of agelessness,
whilst the sows
moan at first glance
of light, peeling back
my lungs,

my stupidity,
my venom for life,
and welcomes me
to a feast of wonts
and needs
and matter
and recklessness
and love that matters.

Anything to get a feed on.

BROTHERHOOD BROKEN

we wallow in the inevitable,
this greying gulf between us,
unreachable these days
as we plod about
with angled feet
whispering for a fresh start.

swallowed up in time,
locked in step from one
frantic moment to the next,
our truths laid naked
and charred to the touch,
our committed brotherhood mangled
and waterlogged
with newfound resentments.

what once
flew through the light
of darkness,
now sinks in a powdered rage
thick with a dizzying array
of self-pity.

SHALLOW GRAVE OF SECRETS

you done dragged me long enough
through pine and soot,
the weight of your relentlessness
has turned my knuckles ruby red
as my eyes spiral and drip dry
while your own beam with heady might.
flogged by your unforgiven heart,
now tethered to my own rank story,
once filled with knowledge,
with worth,
with love,
where the nets grew fat
and the fish sprang to meet each request,
when the heart jumped and rung truth
from bank-to-bank,
now a shallow grave of secrets
and sad songs,
each sung weaker than the next,
brazen, volcanic, crude,
your rich intent,
tattooed cross your shared chest.

MAKING MY WAY TOWARD NOWHERE

With a hat made of leaves
and a chin of metal,
with heavy fumes rising from my stocking feet
and black space between my broken teeth,
I gather my mule and set forth
across prairie and winds,
sleeping 'neath trees,
working for coins,
eating left over beans and coon,
as the buzzards circle the electric sky,
and the sows in the pens
whine with contentment,
the belly bends with worry
as I pace along the horizon,
counting clouds
and memories past,
making my way towards nowhere.

LOUD AND WIDE

Bark loud and wide
Let 'em hear your open sores bleed
As they crowd the bowl around one fountain
And tussle the brow of one love nation
One idea
One fixation
And milk the tit of a thousand empty utters
Lapping at the dried nipple of hope
Of seduction
Of contentment
Calling on the same formations
Same constellations
Same damnations
While I kick at the back door
With grim determination
Never stopping to adore
Never daring to implore
The masses I take no more
Therefore
I stand alone
As you stand with others
Basking in the safety
Of an idea dried up
With opportunity
Bark loud and wide
Let them hear your sores bleed.

TOO FAST TOO SOON TOO MUCH

Swallowed by sunlight,
our tiger jaws feeding off one another,
basking in imperishable delight,
two sows with clasped hands
kneeling at the Alter of Love.

It was bliss....till it wasn't.
Till the trowel scrapped bottom,
Till our kisses turned slender,
Till our logic swam crooked strokes
against the deflating tides along the shore.

We hung on, dearly
and by our chewed fingertips
we dug in and dug out
each swaying beyond dimension,
once vast and plump,
now skeletal, fragmented,
the result of passions overindulgence.

Too much, too soon,
we feasted on our days
and nights till the trough was empty
and we ignored
all others around us --
our soldiers, our loved ones,
our wits and hallucinations,
our own heated denials.

And by April, our love was
buried with the rest
in a flaming pit of humility
and loss.

Too fast, too soon, too much.

LATHER MY BONES IN TAR

Squelched, that's how I feel,
rubbed out and achy with fragility.

Boom! I'm back and ready to take
on all prisoners,
ready to make love
to a hundred sonnets,
ready to lather my bones in
memories of gold.

Dang, I'm down again.
I can't get out of bed.
My tongue has thickened with lies
as I roll about in tar and weep
lonely on a graveled road.

Wow! I feel great, like a beast,
like something from a Marvel comic.
Look at my muscles peak,
look at the cut of my jaw,
look at the words I push from my
cratered mind.
Oh, darn, back again, licking the curb.
Dour and saddened with this rolling
flame baked ravaging routine
where up is down,
down is up,
and comedy is darker than midnight.

I ride the waves,
I see the whites in their eyes,
I steady myself for my daily breaking points...

And languish in this mote of screaming chameleons.

DON'T ORDER THE CALAMARI

Crashing empty handed into a dirty latrine
somewhere south of Phoenix,
appearing like a doped-up mope
sick from the stick,
my gums lined with dead skin,
my eyes flat with bloodshot redness,
I reach frantically for the flush knob
on the johnnie
and kick at the door behind me.
With one eye open, I read:
"Call Peggy 555-1212"
Not tonight, Peg.
Behind me, I hear the cranked-up voices
far past whispers angling for my throat,
these piss-soaked posers studying
their tongues in the mirrors,
each counting their grievances
against me, sizing me up.

I'm sick, boys. Not a junkie.

And don't order the calamari.

WORDS JUST CAN'T

our words can't breathe
can't fuck
can't lick a face
can't strangle a foe
can't ride with Black Angels

they just can't

our words can't flag a taxi
can't roll a smoke
can't pay an old invoice
can't lay in bed all day
reading Celine

they just can't

our words can't drive to a poetry reading
can't walk out on a tab
can't sucker punch some bar sow
can't worship any Gods

they just can't

our words they can't do many things
they can't call into work
they can't run with the bulls
they can't blow trumpets
they can't bet on the horses
but our words can do many things

they can bring us peace
and work our minds
and grant us stability
and solace
and personal satisfaction
and a widening of our true dimension

that's why we write
for girth
for pity
for nostalgia
for weight

and that's good enough for me.

HAPPY TO SHARE

Forgive me, for I spoke with no restraint.
I spoke a language that confused you.
A language that hurried your anxiety.
A language that manifested inside your wrath.
For that, I am not sorry.
A see the holes in your demeaner,
each struggling to reach
the thinning rays of sunshine,
caste wide across your furrowed brow.
I see you bending your waist
and curling your lips with caution,
hiding from the day's delirious beauty.
I see it, and it bothers me.
Yet, think of me no more,
and stand tall
and strident
and bathe your face in the heat,
in the mire,
in the wilds of your manhood,
and baste in your remorse,
in your regret,
in your inability to worship what is free.

But I'm always happy to share.

SPRUNG FROM A FUNK

You took my tongue,
once tough as shoe leather,
knotted with rust spots,
numb with illness,
and you flushed it clean,
tearing past my tangy teeth,
my smoke-stained gums,
my honeycombed tonsils,
and you soaked the whole vessel clean,
clean as ivory, as marble.
And you did this with goodness
with dignity
with love
with air
as you washed my innards
with corn and barely and bean,
knocking the winter
right out of me.

HUSH AND WAIT

the voice arrives from nowhere
buried far beneath life's cryptic banter
tucked beyond the stars
along the ribs of moonbeams
on the backroads of a galaxy
and this voice beckons us too
uncoil from each sinking afternoon
and begs us to look
beyond the falling sun
and listen and watch
and pace and wait
for a higher calling.

PAUNCHY PONY BOYS

we engulfed him
covered him like a cobra,
our skin latched to his,
a full circle of pony boys
languishing paunchy
at the rim
of the funeral parlor

we were young men,
our truths based in
exaggerations,
this gold star carpet ride
so filled with howling nights,
this allegiance
to one another

we were fatherless now,
one and counting,
a mob of emotions
held court in our hearts
as our friend said goodbye
to a force
not soon forgotten

slowly not knowing,
what else to do,
we surrounded our friend,
bound as one,

a weighted mass of devotion
sprung from our tested pores,
sick with sticky liquor

the huddle ended,
but there's been more
winking at each promised hour
as we inch closer to the rim,
stacking tears
and good times too.

TO DO WITH KINDNESS

To kneel before the demented
and unwashed,
burning flames from their burning minds,
I do so with kindness.

To squander willingness
to meld love and forgiveness
between what's lost and forgotten,
I do so with kindness.

To reach inside a strangers
broken heart on a barren night
swelling with contempt and rot,
I do so with kindness.

To move through a festering crowd
tangled in hateful fears bore out
of a clumsy delusion,
I do so with kindness.

I do so because,
well, I don't know
what else
to do.

POCKETS OF FLESH

the serpent stiffens
out of the bowels
of my belly
and slides headlong
into meaty flesh
twisting and slurping
through pockets of waste

feasting off blood tumors
wrapped in deadened skin
swallowed full of broken bones
now gasps
on clots of soot

the dawns moans for dithering light

each sardonic wiggle
the serpent pokes my bloat
and twists the winds into knots

weeds tumbling inside my eyes
where blackened veins
gallop on my spine
with bent cones
that stagger in fear
on burnt rods
sharpened by knives

the rarest of cries gives birth
to whales of floating corpses
drifting by my windowpane
screeching for my presence
demanding my soul as payment

with nothing to do
no place to wiggle
no harbor to swim against
no values to float upon

I give up and let you feast

now, slobber away, you beast

that's some good eatin'.

BROKEN SHADOWS

Sneezing hard into my wrist
I measure the faces
In the corners of the room
Each covered in bone spurs
With dissidence on their brow
Tongues hung to the floor
Lapping, lapping, lapping
Up the scraps of wisdom
Thrust upon by burned out
Scabs with whiskers curled
Upon their knees
Scarred by delusion
Perfected only by broken mirrors
Clouded with the moans of a generation
Hearty swine sway like zombies
With drink in hand
Eyes gone black
Skin loose and gray
And scream like children
At the first sign of blood
AMATEUR'S!
Return to your corners!
Huddled about with jagged clout
-- the poet, the painter, the sculptor, and fraud --
While sweeping glances
Fall flat upon the broken shadows
Smirking beyond the hedges
Outside.

WET MY GULLET

come hither you delicious tyke
allow me to bathe in your beauty
wash over tongue and jaw
with fragility so sweet

white heated cankers throb
and dissolve with each swallow
one bubble haughtier than the last
crowded laughter chimes truth

the roots of your beginning
christened and blessed in
holy waters as throngs of revelers
belch into the face of the majestic

your powdered face tightens
as our cheeks swell with spiked
tears, legions of them falling
on tiny knees and wrists

bark away, bark you must, young sire
let the angels shiver at your arrival
spill your poison down our gullets
make heaven wait another day

for now, we meet

HIJACKED AT NIGHT

My whole mind
my whole world
for the briefest of days
was consumed with this
wall-eyed woman that spit lies
that grew horns
that seemingly radiated
in the rain
she was full of clouds and whispers
she wore lime colored clothing
her stockings were always torn
her toes smelled of custard
and her lips were tortured with praise
always going on about this
always going on about that
always going on about herself
i grew to love her narcissism
so baked in crashing contradictions
compounded fibs hijacked at night
she would wake up lying
she would wake up in a halt
she would wake up and immediately
launch into a diatribe about all the things
she was going to do that day
but never got around to doing
it grew tired
she grew sour
my face fattened with her lies
her lies lost light

they had no real edge,
no meat on them anymore
then one day,
she was gone
poof, just gone
a ghost
i missed her for a minute
her dirty stocking
and spring-colored blouses
her crossed eyes
and cracked lips dried out by fiction
but every story must end
even the ones filled
with nothing but lies

TO BE HEARD

It's a quest
a quest to be heard
to see if I can do it
to see if I can raise an eyebrow
to mine my way through the fuselage
clogging my winter-bred disposition
to pad my ego
to feed my need
my need to be heard
my quest
to be something
to be anything
even something close to nothing
just to be heard
even once
even if nothing comes out of it

That's how I roll.

YES, SIR.

At least once a week
At the very least
I'm instructed by some sour-faced
gentleman,
that I don't need to call him Sir.
Nonsense, I say, or think,
at the least, as I hold a door
or thank someone
for a rack of beers
or pack of grits:
Thank you, sir.
You don't have to call me, sir.
I don't? Are you sure?
Does my father know this?
Perplexed, they usually shoot me a stare.
How am I to know if you're father knows this?
Oh, because, well, I was raised by a Marine.
Fantastic, happy for you,
they say, or at least think
And if I were to refer to a man or woman
of older age other than Sir or Ma'am
my ass got skinned
So, thank you, sir.
I know I am old enough
to be your father
or your nephew
or your uncle
But no matter the gap,
no matter the size

or spectacle of your might,
from here on out,
grits or no grits,
I will refer to you as Sir.
Where is this Marine you speak of?
I would like to shake his hand
He's dead, sir.
I'm sorry to hear that
Thank you, sir.

TRAIN WRECK

The voice? My head?
It's a train wreck
Today at least
A mosh pit of deniability
A symphony of contradictions
An enemy to my sanity
And I wish it wasn't so
I wish it was a soothing laxative
Cooling the bowels of my brain
I wish it was a warm mouth
To rest my tongue upon
I wish it was a true friend
Not a black-eyed backstabber
Instead, though, my mind
Throws cheap shots
Throws hand grenades
Throws tired words of wisdom into
The pockets of my fears
And I bathe in it, unwillingly
I try, I do, to swim through the currents
To bypass the sharp coral reefs
To rise above the deliberate dementia
But the mind, well, she does as she wants
Ruthless and cunning with her intent
The worst kind of lover
But passionate
So, I stick with her
I have no choice.

EXPECTATIONS

Your expectations I can not meet
Your wanton desires I can not fend off
Your cosmic glow surrenders me to rubble

This is my issue

I'm consumed with your cruelty
I'm shabby in clothes and wisdom
I'm weak and scarred by your exhausting ignorance

But I come back. Always.

Not to your face or fragilities
Not to your mind or stern platforms
Not to your ears eyes or skin

I come back to teeter for hours
On the vibrations of your panicked voice
Desperate cries dissolved in time
On the banks of the limbless

I come back, I always come back
Because I have no place to go.

And neither do you.

PIG SKINNER

there was this young boy
with a smashed in nose
and a hair lip
that revealed but one nasty tooth
jutting out his face.

his daddy was a pig skinner.
the kitchen of his shack was filled
with hanging pig skin.

one day I sees that boy clawing
his way out the riverbank.

his eyes were wild and stricken.

then i sees him dragging his
own body through the bramble
and his legs were bent back and pinned
to his ass, just stuck in place.

he's screaming of course.
and he's using that hanging tooth
to claw his way through the mud and grass.

never seen that before

I SAYS SO

It ain't your time to bleed
That's what she says to me
Fifteen times a day
Words lost in infamy
All chalked up
Bluster and dust
She rails on my ways
Minutes turn to days
I tell her to tuck her tail
Set fire to the sky and just bail
But she don't know my plight
Thinks all I wanna do is fight
She knows nothing of my ways
Caustic and bend, lost in a purple haze
I call out her verdicts
Her mind fucks
And purpose
I try to lead her on
Let her dance to my last song
But she ain't got no flow
Rustled and gnarly, unshaved down below
I can't handle that maze
The button I graze
Hopeless…
Especially when I ain't blazed
I'm as low down as the next
Chronic, wild and willing to flex
So rail on sister, with your wicked lies

Call mama, call pops, call my priest
He's as fucked as the next guy
No leaders in my life
Broke from the start, shut down first light
So you tell me not to fight
Don't wrestle at night
Easy for her to say
Locked down in suburbia
Pilled out with kids to raise
Nah, sister, your mirror is clouded
Cracked down the middle and shrouded
Wipe it clean and see what I see
You as violent as me
That's right, I says so.

BACK OF THE BUGGY

By the time I awoke
In the back of the buggy
We done galloped ourselves
Right into another new town
I didn't know what town it twas'
But Mama seemed happy
She had a tiny smile
Curling 'cross her lips
And Daddy's eyes lit up
Least one of them
And my lil' sister couldn't sit still
Bouncing 'round on the back board
Her new skirt getting caught on penny nails
And the folks looked kind enough
Crossin' the streets in them
New used hats and
Angel skin and
Shoes with no holes in em'
Hiding their white smiling faces
Each looking past us
Knowing the look on
Mama's face
And in Daddy's eyes
And bustling 'round sisters white dress
And these folks knew
Just what I knew
That this town
Like all the other towns

Would be like all the rest
Nickle a day jobs
Meatless soups
Heatless quarters
Promises broken
But I kept it too myself
Cause I like to see Mama smile
And Daddy's eyes shine
And my sister feeling pretty.
I can handle ugly.

Cause I'm young.

THE BEAUTIFUL UNKNOWN

fret not, loving sparrow,
for the gloom you desire
will thrust itself upon you
someday,
sounding like shoes in a dryer
as it bucks at your heart
with wild abandonment,
hellbent on welcoming you
into the Love Club --
a rollicking,
half-mad,
deliriously frustrating endeavor --
filled with chaos and crimson
colored lines of dementia,
thorny and cryptic,
confusing and spiteful,
but in the end,
upon her hungry arrival,
love will bait you in believing
in the unattainable,
and whollup your senses
as you mine your way
around the minutia
before
cleansing your soul
in the beautiful unknown.

FRAUGHT WITH TREACHERY

From my breath to my britches
I plod about on aching knees
confounded by the rank
by the worshipped
by the scoundrel's
feeding off my dire state,
using me as an example
tempting me with flesh
and wages
and promises
as I sway clumsily against
the city's empty streets
convulsing and bucking
with dry heaves as I nuzzle
my faces against winter's wind,
a lamb lost in Eden,
crestfallen and romantic
yet storming towards a confession
only I'm never willing
to share
as a stillness deepens
and the whispers fade
into the hollow
alleys fraught with
treachery.

AND THEN WE TANGO

Inside is worse
full of cavities
nickel sized lesions
and bulbous dark veins
hardening
where fermentation lurks
under my sagging skin
and ties my flabby lips
in a tangle.

But on the outside
my broken elbows shine
my scarred face blinks
my dead eye widens
against the sun
and thrust I must
the widest of smiles
to the wildest of minds
each mired in fantasy.

And then...we Tango.

ROLLING FORCE OF FUNGI

Smelling the skin
on my glowing wrist,
I taste the bone,
its marrow deliciously
resistant.

Behind my eyes
patience weeps, then cuts
upstream towards the salmon
scented Rickenbacker blowing
bubbles below.

My toes, each longer
than the next, dimensionless
faded talons
squirting mouthfuls of pity
into the gardens rust.

My chest, a rolling force
of limpish air, defines
each breath with mixed intent,
that furnace of grief
ripped away by the
tasty fungi.

I treasure your visits.

FROM BING TO PAVAROTTI

I like my piss to burn
I like my mouth to sweat
I like my face to ache
I like my words to dance
My bones to creak
I like my music low and sad
I like my women hot and mad
I like my wine red or white
I miss the days of fight or flight
That's why I loathe Christmas music
It takes the heat out of my fury
It weakens my viciousness
It takes the kick out of my song
The lust out of my swagger
From Bing to Pavarotti
I hate it all
365 days in a year
And we cut 30-45 days off at the nuts
For what? Winters deserted wonderland?
For what? Seasonal depression?
For what? My empty wallet?
For what? My sadness and solitude?
I loathe all things Christmas
Especially the music
Bar Humbug.

BURNING DOWN THE TOWER

DLZ, step off of me
I know the jive your slingin'
These wicked lines, so sublime
They played behind a scene with Jesse.

The destructive force in which you speak
I know the type, I loathe them freaks
Long toothed games of lies and deceit
I'd rather kick back, roll dice at their feet

I feel the beat, you break it down
But someone's lost, won't be found
You played the game, you run around
Spin the wheel, life's merry-go-round

I carry on as the room falls cold
Consumed and bloated with your endless goals
You used it up, right to the brim
The love I gave, the love grew dim

La, La, La, La
That all you got?
Chiming and rhyming, so full of guts
I've Broken Bad, the trips turned sour
The games, your face, this song

Tonight, I'm burning down this tower.

Rob Azevedo, from Pembroke, NH, is a writer, poet and the host of the radio show "Granite State of Mind" on WMNH in Manchester, NH. He is also the author of the memoir, *Notes From The Last Breath Farm: A Music Junkies Quest To Be Heard*. He published his first book of poetry called *Turning On The Wasp* a couple years back. And now he's hooked.

BLACK DRAGON POETRY SOCIETY

CERTIFIED AND APPROVED

CPSIA information can be obtained
at www.ICGtesting.com
Printed in the USA
BVHW031414161221
624203BV00010B/647